Whadd'ya Gonna Do?

25 Secrets for Getting a Life

Joey O'Connor

Baker Books

A Division of Baker Book House Co
Grand Rapids, Michigan 49516

Published by Baker Books
a division of Baker Book House Company
P.O. Box 6287, Grand Rapids, MI 49516-6287

Paperback edition published 2001

Second printing, February 2002

Printed in the United States of America

Library of Congress Cataloging-in-Publication Data

O'Connor, Joey, 1964–
    Whadd'ya Gonna Do? : 25 secrets for getting a life / Joey O'Connor.
      p. cm.
    ISBN 0-8010-1103-5 (cloth)
    ISBN 0-8010-6358-2 (paper)
    1. High school graduates—Religious life. 2. Young adults—Religious life. 3. High school graduates—Conduct of life. 4. Young adults—Conduct of life. I. Title.
    BV4529.2.O26 1995
    248.8′3—dc20   95-33147

This book is dedicated to all the college-age adults Krista and I have had the privilege of sharing our lives with the past few years. Too many to name, each one of you has a special place in our hearts.

Joey O' Connor draws his insights from his experiences as one of seven rambunctious siblings and as a church youth director for ten years in Laguna Niguel, California. Presently working for Trinet Communications, he is the author of several books: *Breaking Your Comfort Zones and 49 Other Extremely Radical Ways to Live for God; Where Is God When . . . 1001 Answers to Questions Students Are Asking;* and *You're Grounded for Life! and 49 Other Crazy Things Parents Say.*

Contents

Backward Living in a Fast-Forward World

How Do You Define Success?

My family and I had just boarded our United Airlines flight to Honolulu, Hawaii, for a whole week of relaxing in the sun during Christmas vacation. As I settled into my seat, I grabbed the in-flight magazine from the pouch in front of me and began to flip through it.

One thing I like about in-flight magazines is that they're always filled with clever executive toys, interesting products, and unique gadgets I love to look at but never intend to buy. I guess I could purchase the "Vet Approved Training Mat" that zaps twenty thousand volts through your dog if he steps out of the kitchen into the living room, but I don't have a dog. Or I could buy the "Electric Nose Hair Trimmer," but I use the little scissors on my red Swiss Army knife for personal nose grooming. There was also a wide assortment of environmental artwork, exercise machines, luggage bags, computer carrying cases, golf gadgets, and tape series on "Advanced Mega Memory," "Learning Bulgarian Backwards," and "The Secrets of Offshore Wealth Building." Most of the stuff was nothing but a bunch of clever, expensive junk.

One advertisement that caught my eye, though, was a colorful layout of motivational "success" posters. I held the ad close to my face to get a better look. Glossy, large poster prints of quiet, moonlit sand dunes, deep blue-and-white churning waves, golden early morning sunrises, breaching whales, determined rock climbers, and daring snow skiers leaping off snow-covered cliffs were accented with bold motivational quotes surrounded by a thick black border.

ATTITUDE. CHALLENGE. RISK. GOALS. OPPORTUNITY. TEAMWORK. COMMITMENT. SUCCESS. Inspiring words we'd all like to live by covered each poster with a specific challenge to squeeze the most out of every difficulty, opportunity, or danger. Those beautiful pictures and awe-inspiring quotes made me feel strong, powerful, successful, and invincible. I wanted to walk straight up to the cockpit and order the captain, "Move aside, I'll be flying today." A slight nudge woke me out of my daydream, however, as my wife handed me Ellie, our eight-month-old daughter, and said, "Here. It's your turn to change her."

From dreams of success to stinky diapers. It's amazing how quickly the realities of life can dampen our enthusiasm and motivation for success. You'll probably never see any dirty diapers on a motivational poster, but neither will a motivational poster make you a success in life. True success in life is found in pursuing what really matters, and what really matters in life is an intimate relationship with God.

Graduating from high school is an important step toward success in life, but graduating with God is a giant step, a step that fewer and fewer students seem willing to take. After ten years of youth ministry, and attending more high school graduations than I can count, I've witnessed more students graduate *from God* instead of graduating *with God*. I can picture in my mind the names and faces of tons of teenagers who abandoned their relationship with God after high school to chase after the world's distorted definition of success. It's scary and sad. It has caused me to take a deeper look at my relationship with Christ and led me to write this book.

This book is intended to help you discover what true success is—from God's perspective. It's written to help you keep your love for God alive after high school. In it, you'll find dozens of true stories about young people, friends of mine, who struggled and sought to live by God's standards for success. This isn't a book about going to college, how to pick a roommate, find a job, or balance your checkbook. There are dozens of books like that already. Though you'll find a wide variety of topics and themes about life after high school in here, the primary purpose of this book is to encourage you, to deepen your roots in Christ, to show you the relevance of God's Word in every circumstance, and to challenge you to take daily steps walking in God's love and grace for you.

In the past few years, there's been a lot of negative coverage about the Baby Busters and Generation X. The media pundits and critics make it sound like Generation X is doomed! I don't believe that. Throughout history, God's people, in one generation after another, have encountered hardships, difficulties, and struggles, yet God's Word and his promises remain unchanged. As you go through life after high school, my prayer is that you will experience the richness of God promised in Psalm 100:5: "For the Lord is good and his love endures forever; his faithfulness continues through all generations." When you're feeling hopeless, discouraged, and clueless about what to do with your life, I pray you'll hang onto the hope found in Jeremiah 29:11: " 'For I know the plans I have for you,' declares the LORD, 'plans to prosper you and not to harm you, plans to give you hope and a future.' "

God doesn't promise you success like the world does, but then again, this world never keeps its promises. *God always keeps his promises.* If you desire to keep your friendship with Jesus alive and growing after high school, you've taken the first giant step to true success. And you didn't even have to change any dirty diapers!

> May he give you the desire of your heart and make all your plans succeed.
>
> Psalm 20:4

The
Dangerous Side
of Freedom

Checking Your Spiritual Dipstick

The Story

It was my freshman year of college and I was home for Christmas break. Tom, a buddy of mine, and I had made plans to go skiing for the day and we couldn't wait to hit the slopes. His mom said we could borrow the family's puke-orange-colored, four-door Toyota station wagon. All we had to do was make sure we didn't roll it off the mountainside and bring it back with a full tank of gas. No problem.

I spent the night at Tom's house. We woke up at 5:30 A.M. and began our two-hour drive to the Snow Valley ski resort. The first hour went fine as we listened to music and munched on donuts. The second hour was a different story. As soon as we started up the twisting mountain road, Tom's Toyota began to sputter and smoke. Pulling over into the slow lane, we wondered what was wrong.

"The car has been running fine," Tom said. "I don't know what the problem could be."

Slower and slower we crawled up the hill. We had plenty of gas, but the car had absolutely no power. A gas station soon appeared and we pulled inside.

"I don't know a thing about cars," the teenage attendant said. "I just pump gas. The mechanic isn't here."

The slopes were only ten minutes away and the moguls were calling us, so we decided to push on and take care of the car later. Bad decision.

The skiing was great. Tom and I had a blast. Took lots of pictures. Avoided thinking about the car. We left the slopes at 3:00 P.M.; the car started right away and, to our surprise, it was running better than before. For about ten minutes.

Again, smoke started snaking out from under the hood. We slowed to 15 mph until we reached the bottom of the mountain. Finally, we pulled into a real gas station with a real mechanic. The mechanic popped the hood, checked the oil, looked around, peeked his head over, and said, "When's the last time you put oil in here? Your dipstick ain't got a drop on it. You're completely out of oil. You probably cracked the engine block."

The Secret

> Live as free men, but do not use your freedom as a cover-up for evil; live as servants of God.
>
> 1 Peter 2:16

We fried that car! Two quarts of oil would have made the difference between getting home and spending the night at my sister Carolyn's dorm room at U. C. Riverside. It would have made the difference between a simple solution and three thousand dollars for a new engine block.

The secret to success after high school is not frying your relationship with God. It's knowing how to look under the hood of your life and see when it's time to add a couple quarts of oil. It's paying attention to the danger signals of smoke, red warning lights, and a sputtering spiritual life. It's called checking your spiritual dipstick. Knowing when your relationship with God is on the verge of cracking (like Tom's engine block) can mean the difference between simple spiritual maintenance and costly repairs filled with guilt and regret.

Graduating from high school offers you all sorts of new freedoms. You're used to parents, teachers, coaches, and bosses constantly telling you what to do. Now that you're a graduate, eighteen years old, a legal adult, nobody can tell you what to do. You're free! Well, sort of. Nobody can tell you what to do except your parents (who probably still pay for a lot of things), the U.S. government, any company you owe a bill to, your college teachers, military drill sergeant, college coaches, and new bosses. Other than that, nobody can tell you what to do.

God is probably the only one in your life right now who's not going to tell you what to do. Because he loves you, he gives you complete freedom in your relationship with him. You are free to keep walking with him or not. You are free to grow closer to him or not. You are free to follow his ways or not. You are free to add a couple quarts of oil to keep your relationship with God alive or not.

You can experience freedom in Jesus Christ every day or you can fry your relationship with God after high school. The challenge of freedom is to choose freedom in Jesus Christ every day. That's a decision I hope you'll make. It's a decision God hopes you'll make. Graduating with God means living in freedom. What a challenge. What a life. The choice is yours. Don't forget to check those spiritual warning lights—yours or the ones on your friend's mom's car!

The Step

What kinds of freedoms do you have now that you didn't have in high school? How are these new freedoms challenging to you? Write down what your relationship with God was like during your high school years. How can your new freedoms affect your relationship with Jesus? What kind of spiritual maintenance keeps your love for God alive? How can you make your relationship with God your top priority over the coming weeks and months?

Even God Surfs the Net

The Story

"A Boeing 747 thunders across the sky, some 45,000 feet above the Earth. The intercom crackles to life. *'Good evening, ladies and gentlemen. This is your pilot, Captain Trout Fishing in America...'* The rest of the announcement is drowned out, of course, as the passengers shriek madly and try to pry the plane's doors open" (*Los Angeles Times,* March 14, 1994).

Such is the scenario envisioned by a reporter who interviewed a seventeen-year-old by the name of Peter Eastman Jr. of Santa Barbara, California, who recently read a book by that title and enjoyed it so much that he decided to change his name. Legally. After talking with his parents, Peter Eastman Jr. marched down to the county courthouse and came out—yes, that's right—Trout Fishing in America. His dad even paid the $182 fee. Captain Trout Fishing in America.

Can you imagine your father with a name like that? How would you introduce him to your friends? *This is my dad, uh, Mr. America.* Is his first name "Trout" or "Trout Fishing"? What is he going to call his children? *Marlin Fishing in America? Spear Fishing in America? Shark Fishing in America? Made in America?*

Peter Eastm—er, Trout Fishing in America has dreams of becoming a pilot and is close to receiving his pilot's license. Since changing his name, he has been inundated by radio programs, talk shows, and newspapers eager to understand why he changed his name. In his own words, he said, "I just don't see why a person can't be named Trout Fishing in America without it being such a big deal. It seems we are all trapped in just one frame of mind. We have closed our minds to new ideas, and that is not good." Trout Fishing in America is right. I'm going to change my name to a book title I like: *Whadd'ya Gonna Do?* What's your new name going to be?

The Secret

> The man who enters by the gate is the shepherd of his sheep. The watchman opens the gate for him, and the sheep listen to his voice. He calls his own sheep by name and leads them out. When he has brought out all his own, he goes on ahead of them, and his sheep follow him because they know his voice.
>
> John 10:2–4

When I was in high school, the big rage was getting a fake ID card. Juniors and seniors in high school used them to get into dance places, buy beer, and make themselves appear to be older. Before the U.S. government created the high-tech, 3-D, hologram driver's license stamped with a big red "NOT TWENTY-ONE UNTIL 1998," all you needed to make a fake ID was a little Whiteout and a typewriter to change your birthdate. Most of the fake ID's I ever saw looked like a recipe for arrest to any wary police officer with normal eyesight. A fake ID usually looked fake. It also gave a false sense of security.

Being the real you after high school is one of the first steps to graduating with God. It means not trying to Whiteout your relationship with God and the things that are most important to you. It's making a commitment to let your ID be rooted in Jesus Christ and not the society around you.

17

You can change your name, make a fake ID, but you can't Whiteout your life. There's no security in trying to be someone you're not.

Regardless of what your name is, God knows the real you. It doesn't matter if your name is Trout Fishing in America, The Wizard of Oz, or Clifford the Big Red Dog. God's not a heavenly highway patrolman, but he does know if you're living with a fake ID. You can move away, change your name, grow a goatee, pierce your belly button, get a few tattoos, tummy tucks, liposuctions, toupees, hair implants, and costume changes. You can change everything about yourself, but he still knows the real you.

One of the challenges of leaving high school is leaving with the real you. Moving away to a new city or state with all sorts of new freedoms and meeting new people who know nothing of your old life presents the tempting opportunity to be someone you're really not. You can wander off in search of yourself and never find who you're looking for. You can even log onto cyberspace and pretend to be someone you're not, but even God surfs the net. Encrypted computer codes can't fool God. Passwords don't fool God. God still knows the real you.

You can live as the real you by beginning your new life as an adult with a sense of who God wants you to be. You can offer your life to him every day and ask him to create in you the person he has designed you to be. You can continue to follow Jesus after high school, allowing him to be your shepherd, your friend, and your guide. Or you can choose to live with a fake ID. Jesus knows your name and you know the sound of his voice. Following him is the secret to finding yourself. Pretending you don't know God or that you don't need him, for whatever reason, is like whiting out God from your life. It's like changing your name to a silly book title.

The Step

What do you like about yourself? What are the good qualities you see in yourself that are worth keeping after high school? What are the benefits of being in a new environment (like a new school or job) and the positive changes you can make? In what ways could you be tempted to be someone you're not? What negative consequences could you face by trying to be someone you're not? Take a few minutes to write down how you'd like Jesus to lead you after high school. Pray and ask God for the wisdom to always be the real you in every situation.

Living Life Like You're in Charge

The Story

Imagine yourself lying in bed a year or two after your high school graduation. It's 8:30 A.M. and your clock radio just blasted you out of a wonderful, relaxing sleep. Your warm sheets and thick blankets make you feel like sleeping in till at least 11:30. You moved out of your folks' house some time ago. Your roommates have already split for work or class. It's just you. You're home alone and completely in charge. As the clock radio drones on, your brain begins to get bombarded with a spinning plethora (a choice postgraduate word) of thoughts, questions, choices, and ideas about what to do with your day. Since you're in charge of your life, you get to decide what you want to do today. Large cartoon thought bubbles form about your mangled bed-head as you perplexingly wonder, Should I . . .

- Go to the library and finish that English Lit report?
- Divide the phone bill three ways and pay all my over-due bills?
- Go to the beach or a nice park? (It sure is nice out today.)
- Look for that new job I've been wanting?
- Clean this messy bedroom?
- Balance my checkbook?

- Go to the gym and work out?
- Get my car fixed?
- Blow off my afternoon classes? (I always fall asleep anyway!)
- Help my friends with their statistics homework?
- Read my Bible?
- Begin studying for midterms?
- Go back to sleep? (Now there's a great idea!)

The Secret

His master replied, "Well done, good and faithful servant! You have been faithful with a few things; I will put you in charge of many things. Come and share your master's happiness!"

Matthew 25:23

I know this may sound ridiculously obvious (the obvious does tend to elude us!) or just plain stupid, but in case no one has told you yet, YOU ARE IN CHARGE OF YOUR LIFE! If you're a very organized, efficient, and thoroughly responsible individual, you probably don't need to read this chapter. But for the rest of us, including myself, there are certain areas of our lives where we'd just as soon sleep in as often as we could. We tend to drop the ball, leave things unfinished, fail to follow through, totally forget, willfully ignore, conveniently overlook, casually avoid, and allow things to slip through the proverbial cracks. If that sounds familiar, it's time to fill the gap, plug the leak, fix the crack, and unclog the sewerful of excuses you make for your life *. . . you are in charge of your life!*

Freedom is a dangerous thing. That's why I want you to know that you're in charge of your life. You are in complete control of the thoughts, attitudes, decisions, behaviors, and direction of your life. No one can live your life for you. What you choose to do and how you live your life is ultimately up to you. You're in charge.

I love Jesus' parable of the talents in Matthew's Gospel. It's a wonderful story of freedom, choices, and consequences. Three guys were put in charge of their master's property. Each was put in charge of a different amount of money. Two of the guys doubled their master's money, but the third buried his. He knew his master gave him complete freedom to invest the money however he wanted to, but because he was scared, he stuck the money in a hole.

Because the first two servants were faithful with their master's money, the master rejoiced and was glad to put them in charge of many things. The third servant invested nothing. He received nothing. He was called worthless and thrown out of his master's house. Which servant do you want to be like?

Being in charge of your life doesn't mean that you pop off like a rugged, egotistical, individualist. It doesn't mean that you don't need others. It doesn't mean that you can't be dependent on others from time to time. Being in charge of your life means that you accept God's challenge to make something of your life. Your life is dependent on God, yet you accept the positive or negative consequences for every decision you make. *You invest in your life . . . the life God has put you in charge of.* You seek to make a positive return in other people's lives. You understand the importance of investing in your relationship with God. Whatever you do, you live as a faithful servant to the Lord, knowing that some day you're going to be asked about who and what you invested in. You're going to be asked who was in charge of your life.

The Step

What areas of your life do you tend to let slide? What part of your life would you prefer not to be in charge of? What major responsibilities are you avoiding in your life right now? If you're not taking charge of your life like God has intended you to, there's no day like today to start. Make a commitment this week to work on one area of your life that nobody can be in charge of except you.

Now That's a Poor Excuse

The Story

Most church bulletins are pretty boring. Yet they're not as useless as they may seem. Though hundreds of thousands are thrown into the trash every Sunday (a serious environmental no-no), church bulletins are quite useful for creating stealth bomber paper airplanes to throw from the balcony, doodling, copying funny sermon stories, and looking for strange church words like narthex. Occasionally something truly original pops up in print. One Sunday while doodling I discovered this brilliant piece:

No Excuse Sunday

To make it possible for everyone to attend church next Sunday, we are going to have a special "No Excuse Sunday." Cots will be placed in the foyer for those who say "Sunday is my only day to sleep in." We will have steel helmets for those who say "The roof would cave in if I ever came to church." Blankets will be furnished for those who think the church is too cold, and fans for those who say it is too hot. We will have hearing aids for those who say "the priest speaks too softly," and cotton for those who say he preaches too loudly. Score cards will be available for those who wish to list the hypocrites present. Some relatives will be in attendance for those who like to go visiting on Sundays. There will be TV dinners for those who can't go to church and cook dinner too. One section will be devoted to trees and grass for those who like to see God in nature. Finally, the sanctuary will be decorated with both Christmas poinsettias and Easter lilies for those who have never seen the church without them.

The Secret

This day I call heaven and earth as witnesses against you that I have set before you life and death, blessings and curses. Now choose life, so that you and your children may live and that you may love the LORD your God, listen to his voice, and hold fast to him. For the LORD is your life, and he will give you many years in the land he swore to give to your fathers, Abraham, Isaac and Jacob.

Deuteronomy 30:19–20

Choices or excuses? I like that church bulletin piece because it exposes our spiritual laziness for what it is. I'm amazed at how some Christians discipline themselves to wake up before dawn to go surfing, skiing, or exercising at the gym; to be on time for work, business appointments, Monday Night Football, Seinfeld, and soap operas; to study for exams, ACTs, or GREs; but when it comes to going to church, reading the Bible, or going to a Bible study, a truckload of excuses backs up in the driveway with every imaginable reason why it's impossible to include God in their schedule. Instead of being honest by saying, "No, I am choosing not to go to church today," their excuses come pouring out like scummy water from a busted pipe. Often, our choices are nothing but poor excuses.

Your recent graduation from high school presents you with all sorts of new freedoms. You are in charge of your time, your schedule, your priorities, your decisions, your choices. And your excuses. Freedom brings choices. Your most important choices reflect your highest priorities. Your highest priorities will reflect your most valued commitments.

You'll probably never make excuses for your most important choices. If shooting baskets to improve your free-throw percentage is important to you, you'll never say you're sorry for spending three hours a day in the gym. If staying up all night studying to get straight A's is important to you, you won't apologize for that. It's the choices that are lowest on your priority list that you might be tempted to make excuses for. Like going to church. Or spending time alone with God. Or serving someone in need.

One choice you'll never have to make excuses for after high school is making a daily decision to follow Jesus Christ. Putting God first in your life, even at the cost of an "A" or a missed free throw, is something you'll never have to apologize for. You see, we live and die by our choices. Excuses only reveal our weaknesses. Choosing God and his plan for eternal life is the best choice for excuse-free living. Just as God gave the Israelites complete freedom to follow him, God gives you the choice to grow closer to him or not. If at some point after high school, you discover that God isn't number one on your priority list, just be honest and admit it. At least you won't be making a poor excuse.

The Step

Whether your relationship with God is growing or going nowhere, being honest and authentic is the first step to spiritual maturity. Too many people hide behind spiritual masks, afraid to reveal that their lives are not going as well as others think. The most important step you can take in your relationship with God and others is to be authentic. Be honest. Don't make excuses for your life. Be the real you and allow God to help you work through the times when you feel like making excuses in your relationship with him.

Developing a Character
of Credibility

The Story

In my blue, two-drawer file cabinet I have a file in which I hope I never appear. I've labeled it my "has-been" file. In it are numerous newspaper clippings, stories, and names of people who have gone down in flames. People whose reputations and characters have been permanently tarnished by poor moral choices. Want a peek inside?

Millionaire boxer Mike Tyson. Darryl Strawberry. L. A. Kings owner Bruce McNall. Michael Jackson. Yes, even O. J. Simpson. More than a few religious leaders. Even some personal friends whose choices have devastated not only their lives, but also the lives of those closest to them. All of these people, some famous, some not, have one thing in common: a crisis in character.

"Character," wrote the great evangelist D. L. Moody, "is who you are in the dark." Character is your true inner self known only to God and yourself. It is not who others say or think you are; it is the "you" only you really know. My has-been file is a reminder to me of people whose lives were filled with talent and promise, but who chose to throw it away for temporary pleasure. Money. Sex. Power. Drugs. Workaholism. Chasing pleasure, power, or prestige at the cost of character is a high price to pay. It's too high for me to pay. I can't afford it. Neither can you. Let's both avoid winding up in my has-been file.

The Secret

> For this very reason, make every effort to add to your faith goodness; and to goodness, knowledge; and to knowledge, self-control; and to self-control, perseverance; and to perseverance, godliness; and to godliness, brotherly kindness; and to brotherly kindness, love. For if you possess these qualities in increasing measure, they will keep you from being ineffective and unproductive in your knowledge of our Lord Jesus Christ.
>
> 2 Peter 1:5–8

Developing a character of credibility is a lifelong process, one to be taken very seriously. Ultimately, the only thing you have to show for yourself is your character. Character is what counts most. Good looks don't count. Personality doesn't count. Having wealthy parents doesn't count. Brains. Achievements. Awards. Everything associated with success doesn't amount to a filthy pile of stinking trash if there's something in your character that doesn't smell right. D. L. Moody was right: "Character is who you are in the dark." Does your character reflect the light of God's character?

As an early disciple of Jesus, Peter was known for his unpredictable, wild character. Nobody ever knew what Peter would say next. Peter, the one Jesus called a "rock," crumbled; he even denied Jesus three times. After being restored in his relationship with Jesus, however, Peter had an even deeper understanding of God's grace. He understood the importance of character.

Peter had a strong desire to see other Christians develop a character of credibility. He wanted his friends to have effective, productive, and successful relationships with Jesus Christ. That's why he focused on helping his friends add to their faith the character qualities of Jesus, qualities like goodness, knowledge, self-control, perseverance, godliness, kindness, and love. These are qualities you can't live without. It's impossible to develop a character of credibility without them.

Developing a character of credibility is what true success is all about. A Christlike character will always shine through the dark. You'll never regret the cost. You'll never be a has-been.

The Step

Character Carving

Developing a character of credibility is a giant step to growing in your relationship with God. In the coming months, how would you like God to carve your character? How would you like others to see the character of Christ in you? As you count the cost of following Jesus, remember that character counts.

Goodness

How can you apply goodness to your thoughts, motives, intentions, and desires?

Knowledge

How does growing in your knowledge of God develop your character?

Self-control

How can you give the Holy Spirit control of your life every day?

Perseverance

In what area of your life are you being challenged to persevere?

Godliness

How can you be godly in every thought and action?

Kindness

How can you show compassion and sensitivity to others?

Love

How can you receive and give God's love away?

Five Secrets
to
Spiritual Success

6

Prayer Isn't a Foreign Language

The Story

One summer while I was in college, my father, my brother Neil, and I went to Europe for three weeks. Four countries. Three weeks. Italy. Switzerland. Austria. Germany. We weren't exactly the Three Musketeers; we probably looked more like the Three Stooges as we rushed to every plane, train, and soap-box-derby-size-rental car imaginable.

After our first stop in Rome for a few days, we rented a car and headed to Florence. But first we had to try to figure out how to leave Rome without getting ourselves killed. Have you ever seen or traveled on a European roundabout? They are the black holes of transportation design. Picture eighteen streets dumping into one huge swirling mass of cars going around in circles. The powerful gravitational force sucks you into the roundabout vortex, making exiting impossible. Zipping cars are layered eighteen deep. You're fending off moped riders left and right. Horns are blaring. Brakes screeching. It took us two-and-a-half days to exit our first roundabout.

Map in hand, I was co-piloting when my dad finally pulled alongside the curb. "Joey, ask that guy how to get out to the freeway."

"Dad, look at him. He's Italian . . . he doesn't speak any English."

"Go ahead, just ask him."

"Okay, Dad, but I'm telling you he doesn't speak English."

Leaning my head out the window, I asked the man in my best Italian-American accent, "Excuse me sir, do you know how to. . . ."

"No speakeea-lee-inglish," he blurted out. (Told you so, told you so!)

My father then resorted to the ultimate in American ethnocentrism: *If at first you don't succeed, just speak louder and clearer.*

"Doo youuu knnoow hoow tooo geeet tooo theee freeewaaayyy?"

The Secret

And pray in the Spirit on all occasions with all kinds of prayers and requests. With this in mind, be alert and always keep on praying for all the saints.

Ephesians 6:18

There will be times during the next few years that you may feel like you're in a black hole of confusion and doubt—call it a spiritual roundabout. Learning the language of prayer can steer you in the right direction.

Talking with God is the language of prayer. Talking with God is not about sounding holy or coming up with the right words to approach the Almighty. It's about being honest with God about what's on your heart. It's sitting down alone with God and talking with him just like you would with a trusted friend over a cup of coffee. Prayer is the kind of conversation where you don't have to say a thing and God will still understand.

Last year, my wife Krista gave birth to our second daughter, Ellie. The excitement and joy of a quick, healthy delivery was quickly dispelled by the alarming news that Ellie was having breathing problems. When the doctors moved her to the neonatal intensive care unit for observation and testing, Krista and I began to pray. And pray. And pray some more. At first, the doctors said Ellie would only have to spend a couple days in intensive care. Two days turned into four days. Four days turned into a week.

As Krista, our family, friends, and I prayed for Ellie, there were emotionally exhausting times when I was all prayed out. I didn't know what else to say. Or pray. Prayer seemed like a foreign language. Worry and doubt tried to suck me into the cavernous black hole of my worst fears. Just when it looked like Ellie was improving, she'd have another setback. I'd wonder, "Are my prayers working? H-E-L-L-O-O-O! ANYONE OUT THERE?"

Talking with God comes naturally for some. For others, it's like learning a foreign language. Prayer isn't comfortable. You wonder if your prayers evaporate the second they leave your lips. Since prayer is essential to developing your walk with God, do what the foreign language experts say: Immerse yourself in the language you're learning; immerse yourself in prayer.

Paul says a couple very important things to demystify the language of prayer:

1. *Pray in the Spirit.* That means to be dependent on God. Pray with God . . . don't pray at him. Ask God to help you draw out what's bothering you. Read Romans 8:26–27.
2. *Pray at all times.* Whatever's on your mind, pray about it. The way to learn Spanish is to speak Spanish. The way to learn how to pray is to pray. Paul tells us to pray "all kinds" of prayers and requests. Go to God with an

Ephesians 3:12 attitude . . . you can approach God with freedom and confidence.

3. *Be alert . . . keep praying for your Christian friends.* Be alert to opportunities to pray. Seek a friend to pray with. Make the most of every opportunity to learn how to pray. God will steer you out of your spiritual roundabouts.

The Step

Prayer may be a giant step for you, but without talking to God on a regular basis, it's impossible to develop a successful relationship with God. Why don't you find a friend or two that you can begin praying with to learn the language of prayer? Study the following Scriptures together and see how they can shape your prayer life. Meet regularly to pray for one another. Talking with God everyday will make you fluent in no time.

James 5:13–16
Philemon 6
1 Thessalonians 5:17
Luke 18:1–14
Matthew 5:6–13
Colossians 4:2

P.S. Ellie is now a gurgling, smiling baby. She speaks a foreign "ga-ga" language I'm still trying to decipher.

7

Dig Deeper into God's Word

The Story

On Saturday, January 17, 1990, Carrie Heiman and her friends were hiking on a snow-covered hillside in Angeles National Forest when an avalanche suddenly swept them off their feet. Grabbing for trees, branches, each other—anything that would keep them from being buried by the churning, rushing wall of snow—Carrie was quickly buried in an icy grave.

After a quick head count, Carrie's friends realized she was nowhere in sight. While some began to shout and frantically dig to find her, others ran to get help. Soon over eighty students and fifteen chaperones were racing against time and oxygen to find Carrie. Professional ski patrol rescuers arrived twenty minutes later to lead a careful search through the forty-foot-wide and three-hundred-foot-long avalanche debris.

Ninety minutes later, after sticking long avalanche poles into the snow step-by-step, a rescuer near the top of the avalanche debris yelled, "We found her! She's conscious!" Packed deep under the snow, Carrie's frozen body was rapidly uncovered and rushed to the hospital. She was treated for frostbite on her toes and—amazingly—was quickly released from the hospital.

Carrie later explained how she avoided being suffocated. She described tumbling in the snow with her hands on her face. When the wave of snow piled its massive weight on her, Carrie quickly pushed her hands forward. Creating a pocket of air about the size of a basketball, she was able to breathe until the rescuers found her an hour and a half later. Her small pocket of air made the difference between life and death.

The Secret

> I have kept my feet from every evil path so that I might obey your word. I have not departed from your laws, for you yourself have taught me.
>
> Psalm 119:101–2

Digging deeper in God's Word is as vital to your friendship with Jesus Christ as oxygen is to your lungs. Learning to follow Christ by understanding the promises of God provides you that critical pocket of air when the world comes crashing down on you like a roaring avalanche. God's Word gives you Jesus, the Living Word, the source of life you can't survive without.

God shows you the path he wants you to follow. It keeps you from taking the paths of this world, surrounded by avalanches waiting to happen. Why, then, do so many young people stop studying God's Word after high school? Is it boredom? Disinterest? Thinking they know it all already? In Mark 4, Jesus explained to his disciples what can be called the "thorny lifestyle." He told a parable about a farmer sowing seeds and explained that the seed sown among thorns represented the person who hears the word, but "the worries of this life, the deceitfulness of wealth and the desires for other things come in and choke the word, making it unfruitful" (Mark 4:19).

Are you getting choked? Is your relationship with God constantly getting stung by the desire for "other things?"

Digging deeper in God's Word, not just reading or hearing it, but doing what it says, is the true secret to spiritual success. God's Word is the oldest, most reliable book on successful living. But it doesn't offer you success in the way the world defines success. It won't promise to make you rich. It won't guarantee a six-figure income or improve your corporate image. But it will give you what nothing else can: an intimate, dynamic relationship with your Creator. God's Word will lead you to a life of peace. It will breathe life into your heart and spirit when you feel like temptation has got you by the throat. His Word will keep you from every evil path and lead you to everlasting life.

The Step

This week, study Psalm 119. It's the longest psalm and it's all about the wonders of God's Word. In this psalm, you will be able to relate to the many thoughts and feelings expressed in it. Pick one verse to memorize each day this week. Ask God to help you grow in your walk with him by continually growing in his Word.

Don't Be a Lone Ranger Christian

The Story

Steve and I were on a fast blast, a two-and-a-half-day trek across the United States. Earlier that day, I arrived with bloodshot eyes after a late night, cramped seat, no sleep lay-over-in-Chicago-connect-to-Nashville flight. From there we started our trek. Tennessee. Arkansas. Oklahoma (where the wind comes sweeping down the plain). Big, big, big TEXAS. New Mexico. Arizona. California. The Wild West. Steve was heading home after being gone for almost ten months.

Over the past several weeks, Steve had called me a few times to let me know how life was going in Tennessee. By the sound of his voice, I knew life was definitely not going well. In fact, it was horrible. Depressing. Rotten. As Steve explained, he had made one bad decision after another.

After completing his basic training for the Army Reserves in Alabama, Steve began dating a girl he met while visiting his brother in Nashville. When he returned to California a week later, he immediately decided to return to Tennessee to pursue this relationship. After only about six weeks of dating, Steve and his girlfriend began to talk about getting married. Steve moved back to Tennessee. He bought a ring. They got engaged. Three months later, things got messy. Problems with her family. Problems with their relationship. They broke up. Steve was crushed (sound familiar?). Depressed.

Lonely. Never before had he wandered so far away from God, his family, or friends. He decided to come home. Head west. But he didn't want to make the drive all alone. Six states, 2,098 miles. Steve and I had a long time to talk.

The Secret

> Let us hold unswervingly to the hope we profess, for he who promised is faithful. And let us consider how we may spur one another on toward love and good deeds. Let us not give up meeting together, as some are in the habit of doing, but let us encourage one another—and all the more as you see the Day approaching.
>
> Hebrews 10:23–25

Steve's relationship with God began slipping away much earlier than his brief relationship with his fiancée. Before entering the Army Reserves, Steve was baptized on New Year's Day as a public testimony to his commitment to Christ. Only a year later, Steve was farther away from God than he ever imagined he would be. As a high school and college student, Steve was always known for his strong commitment to Christ.

Somewhere around Toadsuck Road, Arkansas, Steve explained how once he got away from home, his relationship with God began to suffer. He spoke of the same common themes I've heard and seen from many other high school graduates. Unfamiliar surroundings. Unfamiliar churches. Lots of distractions. Wondered where to find Christian friends. Tried a couple churches (didn't like them). God seemed distant. Got busy with new lifestyle and friends. God could wait.

Steve's story is a classic example of how a "strong" Christian can end up not only thousands of miles away from home, but a thousand miles away from God after high school. If there's one commitment you make after you graduate, make a commitment to stay in fellowship with other Christians wherever you go. Going it alone with God just doesn't work. Finding a new church, new Christian friends, or a campus Bible study may be hard work, but it's much harder trying to salvage a sunken relationship with God. Without fellowship, it's easy to spiritually starve yourself to death. Lone Ranger Christians don't last very long in the desert.

Finding fellowship provides you with three important things you can't do without in your relationship with God. (1) You receive encouragement; (2) you can become motivated toward love and good deeds; (3) you are challenged not to swerve in your faith. This world will offer plenty of enticements to swerve in your faith if you let it. Just as the writer of Hebrews says, hold on to your hope. Hold on to Jesus wherever you go. Finding fellowship will stimulate you to grow in Christ wherever you are. Don't let your love for God end up like a broken wedding engagement.

The Step

What plans are you actively making right now to find fellowship after high school? Have you begun to pray and ask God to help you find the fellowship you need? If you're staying in your hometown, what young adult or college ministry can you attend? If you're going away to school, what kind of fellowships are offered on campus? Hebrews 10:23 says Jesus is faithful . . . he will provide you the fellowship you need, but you also must be willing to go and find it.

Ten Amazing Words to Impress Your Friends

Zymurgy: the chemistry of fermentation, as applied in brewing.

Yahoo: in Swift's *Gulliver's Travels,* any of a race of brutish, degraded creatures. Usage: *You're a Yahoo.*

Omphaloskepsis: the study of one's belly button. *I can't come to the phone right now; I'm in the process of omphaloskepsis.*

Humahumanukunukuapuaa: the Hawaiian state fish.

Hurdy-gurdy: a musical instrument played by turning a crank. *Crank up the hurdy-gurdy . . . play it loud!*

Kanchenjunga: a 28,146-foot mountain in the Himalayas of Nepal.

Dromedary: the one-humped domesticated camel of northern Africa and western Asia. *Hey Ahmed! Get that dromedary outta here!*

Erratum: an error in a printed text. *This book has only one erratum.*

Querulous: given to complaining; peevish. *Sally is the most querulous girl I know.*

Obiter dictum: an incidental remark or observation said in passing. *One more obiter dictum like that and you're not going anywhere tonight, do you hear me?*

Join God's Secret Service

The Story

During my senior year in high school and my freshman year of college, I helped build a home for orphaned children that still stands today in Maneadero, Mexico. My youth pastor, Todd Temple, had been approached by a Mexican pastor in the streets of Ensenada who asked Todd if he would help him construct an orphanage. What began as a dirt lot along Highway 1 in Baja California is now a thriving complex of buildings, mobile homes, smiling faces, and laughter.

Last year after Christmas, Todd, myself, and a few others of the old construction team got together and headed to Mexico for a visit to the orphanage. As we drove through the orphanage gates, I was amazed at the sight of playground equipment, basketball and volleyball courts, new buildings, and the smell of a fresh cake baked for a child's birthday. We greeted the orphanage director's wife and told her who we were. As she led us on a tour of the facility, my mind flashed back to fond memories of long, hard days mixing cement, digging postholes, and engaging in wild water fights to cool off from the heat. Racing with old memories as we walked from room to room, I thought, *I remember*

*laying this floor. This is where we helped with the roof. This
is the room where we played volleyball before it had a roof.*

Stepping into another room, we were greeted by thirty or
so smiling children who were playing together. Shouts of
"Hola!" and "Dios le bendiga" (God bless you) filled the colorful, mural-painted room. Standing in one of the hallways where
I remember smoothing the cement foundation for hours one
freezing cold night, I saw a beautiful mural of a castle by the
sea built on a huge rock. The wall bore the Spanish transla-
tion of the Bible verse, "Everyone who hears these words of
mine and puts them into practice is like a wise man who built
his house on the rock" (Matt. 7:24). I smiled and thanked God
for building a firm foundation in so many little lives.

The Secret

The man who loves his life will lose it, while the man who hates
his life in this world will keep it for eternal life. Whoever serves
me must follow me; and where I am, my servant also will be. My
Father will honor the one who serves me.

John 12:25–26

If you want to be a true spiritual success, lose your life by
joining God's secret service. Lose your life by giving it away.
There is nothing more meaningful or more rewarding than
building God's kingdom by serving others as Jesus did.

Our society spends enormous amounts of time, energy, and
money pursuing the things it loves. When we visited the
orphanage, it was a cold, windy day. I was wearing an expensive Patagonia fleece jacket with a colorful print design. Since
I have a tendency to lose prized things, I've always fought hard
trying not to lose this jacket. When the director saw me, she
laughed at me and I didn't understand why. She led us to the

boys' dormitory and much to our surprise, all twenty beds were covered with the same Patagonia fleece material. Same color. Same print. Same blanket. The same as my prized jacket. My friends laughed and teased me, "One man's expensive jacket is the same blanket for twenty Mexican orphans." I was rightly humbled.

What do you value and treasure the most? Is it something like my stupid jacket or is it serving others? What are you doing that brings an eternal return in other people's lives? Serving doesn't earn you brownie points from God. It won't make God love you any more or any less, but serving flows from following Jesus. It's a supernatural response to knowing the heart of Jesus. Jesus promises that the Father will honor whoever serves him. What firmer foundation can you possibly have in your life?

The Step

In God's kingdom, serving others is not an option. It's not a legalistic requirement but authentic evidence of Jesus at work in your life. Serving others is the work of the Holy Spirit in your life to change this needy, desperate world. What do you truly value? What lasting legacy are you building for God's kingdom? Where does serving others rank in your priorities and time schedule? If you're not actively involved in some area of Christian service, keep following Jesus and ask him to lead you where you can serve others in his name.

10

Be Contagious with Encouragement

The Story

On the Fourth of July, my wife, my daughter Janae, and I entered a 10k race in Laguna Niguel. The "Run through the Parks" was designed between two city parks with a long, flat stretch alongside a peaceful lake. Since Janae was only eight months old, I did double duty by pushing her the whole ten kilometers in her baby jogger. While she gurgled and went along for the free ride, Krista and I ran at an easy pace, surrounded by a couple thousand runners dressed in assorted patriotic clothing of red, white, and blue.

Once the 10k race began, it was only a few minutes before the gun went off for the start of the 5k race. After forty-five minutes of running around the lake and trying not to run over anyone with the high-tech baby stroller, Krista, Janae, and I were about a half mile from the finish line. Up ahead, I noticed a small group of people heading in our direction. "That's strange," I thought to myself. "The 5k's over and the 10k's almost over; who could possibly still be heading this way?"

As we ran closer, my eyes focused on a small girl in the middle of the three or four adults surrounding her. Only around eight or nine years old, she had braces on her legs and her arms were supported by crutches. In a slow, awkward, clunky rhythm, she stepped forward one leg at a time. One crutch at a time. *She was just starting her race.*

Cheers rang out from the runners who passed her in the opposite direction. "You can do it! Hang in there! You're doing great!" Nudging her along with words of constant encouragement and support, the adults walking alongside supported her every step of the way. As the little girl looked up at the cheering runners passing her, a wonderful smile beamed across her face. When Krista and I ran past, offering our enthusiastic encouragement, a wave of cold, electric chills rushed through my whole body as I admired the strength and bravery of this young, smiling girl. If only every person had the courage of this small child, what an amazing world this would be.

The Secret

As iron sharpens iron, so one man sharpens another.

Proverbs 27:17

I get tears in my eyes almost every time I think of that physically crippled girl running a 5k race with a big smile on her face. When I consider the awesome power of encouragement, I wish every person I know was surrounded by three or four people nudging, motivating, and encouraging him or her to hang in there in this race of life.

Encouragement is a powerful weapon against the temptation to quit the race God has marked out before you. Encouragement empowers you with the courage to keep running despite the obstacles that block your way. No one can live without encouragement . . . *you can't live without encouragement.* It is the breath of life to your heart and soul.

True spiritual success is being contagious with encouragement. When my body was tired and sore after running ten kilometers, my perspective was immediately changed as I cheered the little girl on. Encouragement got my eyes off myself and my pain, and focused me to help her in her struggle. Passing that child in crutches put my pain in perspective pretty darn quick. I felt like a wimp compared to her.

You can have a powerful effect on others by being contagious with encouragement. Your words, support, and actions of love can show your family and friends that you believe in them. When you're contagious with encouragement, you spread a wonderful disease. You sharpen the lives of those around you who have been dulled by pain and discouragement. By encouraging others, you'll get your eyes off yourself and become the support others need. Your words of encouragement will keep others in the race. Your words may be just what someone needs to cross the finish line.

The Step

Your encouragement can make a huge difference in the lives of people who need your support. Take a giant step today and be contagious with encouragement. Cheer someone on by writing a friendly note, making a phone call, or sharing a few kind words. Who needs your encouragement today? Be contagious with encouragement!

Total
Life Focus

Dare to Dream

The Story

One of my favorite books is a true adventure story about a San Francisco reporter named Joe Kane who set out on a South American expedition to raft the entire length of the Amazon River. This city slicker knew absolutely nothing about river rafting, the Amazon, jungle insects, snakes, Marxist guerrillas, narco-traffickers, or paddling technique. You probably know more about rafting than he did.

Starting at the very source of the Amazon River, a small trickle of water somewhere around seventeen thousand feet in the Peruvian Andes, Joe Kane began a six-month journey to raft the entire 4,200 miles. Battling fierce rapids, thousand-foot gorges, terrorist bullets, bad drinking water, insects, personality clashes, and fatigue, this mild-mannered reporter finally completed his dream of paddling the whole Amazon River.

Not only was Joe Kane's story, *Running the Amazon*, exciting to read, it also inspired me. As I read this incredible, danger-filled epic, one thing became very clear to me: Joe Kane wasn't afraid to dream. He wasn't afraid to take risks. Big risks. He wasn't afraid to dream about impossible things no one else had ever done. He wasn't afraid to challenge himself with a new sport he knew nothing about on the world's largest, most dangerous river.

Daring to dream is a personal characteristic you don't find in many people today. There are countless more apathetic people with tepid wishes, lukewarm desires, and unenthusiastic motivations than those rare passionate individuals with dynamic, unpredictable dreams. As I read about Joe Kane's incredible dream to raft the Amazon, it reminded me of the most radical, seemingly impossible dream of all: God sending Jesus Christ to this lost and broken world to bring us back into fellowship with him.

The Secret

> Jesus looked at them and said, "With man this is impossible, but not with God; all things are possible with God."
>
> Mark 10:27

Living a successful life after high school is like attempting to raft the Amazon. The harsh, powerful rapids of life can quickly smash your dreams on the jagged rocks of reality. Life after high school is a long, wild river filled with adventures, risks, dangers, doubts, fears, successes, failures, disappointments, defeats, and dousings. Life is a wild and dangerous river. Especially if you're not properly prepared for the long paddle. That's why you need dreams. Even impossible dreams. Dreams propel you to keep paddling when you feel like giving up. Dreams motivate you to live life like a participant instead of a spectator. Dreams give you meaningful direction instead of purposeless wandering. The quality of your journey in life will reflect the quality of your dreams.

What kind of daring dreams do you have for life after high school? How are you stepping out in faith with impossible dreams for God? What types of risks are you taking for Jesus Christ? By what radical standard are you living your life? Are you ready to begin living your life with impossible dreams that only God can make possible? Dreaming for God is looking at the way things are and saying, "Lord, how do you want to pull off the impossible here? How do you want me to be a difference-maker for you?"

I believe Jesus Christ was a wonderful dreamer rooted in reality. He saw life as it was, but he lived life as it is supposed to be lived. Jesus wasn't a pathetic, hopeless dreamer. His life, his attitude, his dream, and vision radically challenged what every skeptic and critic in his day thought was ridiculous and impossible. Jesus dreamed of setting this world free from sin and death. Because he wanted to restore mankind's relationship to his Father, people nailed him with all sorts of horrible, vicious insults. Hordes of critical, unbelieving cynics tried to steal his dream: *You're a dreamer, carpenter boy! A deluded Galilean geek! You're a demon-possessed dork!*

When you dare to dream great dreams for God, you stand to get ridiculed just like Jesus. Friends won't always understand your dreams. Parents may criticize your dreams. Your teachers will say getting higher grades are more important than your dreams. The bigger your dreams are, the louder your critics will cry. Don't allow other people's criticisms to crush your dreams. Only you can make your dreams happen. Nobody else has your dreams. Nobody else has your life to live. Live your life by following your dreams and not someone else's criticism. The people who criticize you most are usually the ones who abandoned their own dreams years ago. Watch out for dream stealers. Commit your dreams to God and let him live out the awesome adventure he has planned for you.

The Step

What have you dared to dream about lately? Do your dreams include God or do they leave him deep in the Amazon jungle? Dreaming impossible things for God after high school is a giant step to success because too many young people are afraid to dream great things for God. When you begin dreaming great things for God, I believe you'll experience an unimagined richness and closeness with your Creator. Write down two or three dreams you have for your future. Give your dreams to God today and pray about them on a regular basis. Share your dreams with an encouraging person who will believe your dreams with you!

Design Your Life Purpose

The Story

You're sick of it by now. For the past six months, everyone from your greying grandmother to your bald-headed boss to your gabby hairstylist to your intrusive aunts and "Atta-boy" uncles to the guy who works at 7–Eleven to your inquisitive parents have been asking you the same stupid question: "So, whadd'ya gonna do after you graduate from high school?" *(The next person who asks you that question is gonna get a mortarboard right in the kablooey!)*

What is your typical, socially acceptable response to that question? It usually lands somewhere between (A) school (B) work (C) the military (D) travel and see the world (E) all of the above (F) none of the above.

Pick F. Blow the inquiring minds in your life away with these eyebrow-raising-"I-see"-quickly-turn-and-head-to-the-chip-bowl-sorry-I-asked-looks-of-confusion-on-their-faces responses.

- I'm joining an elite French paramilitary squad to fight tooth decay.
- I'm commuting between Stanford and M.I.T. to work on dual bio-chemistry degrees with an emphasis in personal flotation devices.

- Nothing, why do you ask?
- I'm planning on sitting in the bottom of a pickle barrel to contemplate my navel . . . I believe I can start a new world religion this way.
- HERE'S A STORY . . . OF A LOVELY LADY . . . WHO WAS LIVING WITH THREE VERY LOVELY GIRLS . . . ALL OF THEM HAD HAIR OF GOLD . . . LIKE THEIR MOTHER . . . THE YOUNGEST ONE IN CURLS!!!

The Secret

> With this in mind, we constantly pray for you, that our God may count you worthy of his calling, and that by his power he may fulfill every good purpose of yours and every act prompted by your faith.
>
> 2 Thessalonians 1:11

It was a silly question to even ask in the first place. Once your friends and relatives get over the shock of your, hm, well, interesting response, it's probably worth your time to start thinking about your purpose in life. Whadd'ya think?

One thing that has always captivated me about Scripture is the exciting discovery I made as a teenager when I learned that God had a purpose for my life. Have you ever stopped to think that the God of this universe has a unique purpose for your life? Living your life on purpose, according to God's purposes, is the secret to true success after high school. And into eternity. Check out what Webster says purpose is all about:

Purpose: To intend or plan-*n.* 1. something one intends to get or do; aim 2. determination 3. the object for which something exists or is done—on purpose intentionally—purposeful *adj.*—purposeless—*adj.*

Which adjective best describes your life? Is your life *purposeful* or *purposeless*? How do you *intend* to live your life? How do you *plan* on living your life after high school? Are you *determined* to live by God's ways or your own ways? Are you *intentional* in the important "life decisions" you make? And here's the big one, the MOTHER OF ALL AFTER-HIGH-SCHOOL QUESTIONS: *Why do you exist? What is your purpose in life?*

Asking yourself, "What is my purpose in life?" is a question many young people avoid because they're afraid of discovering that their life has had little or no purpose at all. Without the deep security of knowing that God has a definite purpose for your life, it's easy to throw yourself into loads of meaningless activity trying to create a self-constructed sense of purpose. Finding your purpose rooted in an intimate and personal relationship with Jesus Christ provides a solid, stable foundation for your life. That's the kind of foundation you can't afford to live without.

I love the concern Paul has for his Christian friends. He was constantly praying for them to find their purpose rooted in their relationship in Christ. Paul affirms God's work in their lives by sharing three important reminders:

1. You have been called by God. God has specifically chosen to have a growing, lasting relationship with you. That means a growing, deepening relationship with him even after high school. You have been called by God. That's the highest calling you could ever desire to live for.

2. You have a purpose. By his power, God wants to fulfill every good purpose in your life. That's amazing! There are so many people walking around today with no sense of purpose or direction in their lives. In Jesus Christ, your life can be different. You can live with purpose, satisfaction, and meaning by following God's dynamic design for you.

3. You have an active faith. I can't think of a more meaningful way to live than living out your faith by making an active difference in the lives around you. You are surrounded by opportunities to live a purposeful life. Your faith is not a dead, useless relic, but an alive, active agent for God's purposes. God promises that every act prompted by your faith in him will make an eternal difference. If that's not living life on purpose, I don't know what is.

The Step

Designing your life purpose begins with rooting your identity in Christ.

You don't have to make any crucial career decisions to discover your purpose in life. All you have to do is begin to ask God how to live according to his purposes. As you live by God's ways, your relationship with God will flow into anything you choose to do. Start where you are right now. For who you are today, what is your purpose in life? What might be God's purposes for your life right now? How can you begin living your life on purpose today?

Develop Your Life Mission Statement

The Story

During high school, Jeff was always one of those steady, consistent guys I could count on. In fact, he was one of the very first guys in the youth ministry. He went on almost every youth ministry trip and influenced a number of friends for Christ. During the summers, he worked as a water-ski boat driver for a popular camping ministry. Jeff always found time to be involved in Bible studies, serving, and helping others to grow in their faith. The one thing Jeff didn't do was waver in his faith. He was steady, consistent, and dependable. In high school.

After graduation, Jeff wandered through his first two years of junior college. He wasn't too thrilled about his classes, a number of good friends had gone away to other colleges, and overall, Jeff's life (by his admission) wasn't very exciting. Including his relationship with God.

Jeff experienced all sorts of mixed emotions and experiences after high school. The party scene began to look attractive, so he began experimenting with alcohol. His regular church involvement dwindled down to going to services whenever he felt like it (every other Tibetan New Year.) Overall, as Jeff described it, his relationship with God stank.

After experiencing a severe case of spiritual atrophy (like a weak girlie-man), Jeff finally blasted out of his spiritual complacency and directionless wandering. Tired of living without passion or purpose, Jeff sat down and developed a life mission statement. Soon after came radical changes. I've never seen someone become so focused, so purpose-oriented, so quickly. Jeff's life mission statement launched him into living his life on purpose.

The Secret

> I, even I, have spoken; yes, I have called him. I will bring him, and he will succeed in his mission.
>
> Isaiah 48:15

So what's a life mission statement? A life mission statement is a simple strategy for personal success. It's your personal declaration of who you are, what's most important to you, and what you want to make of your life. A life mission statement summarizes your values, beliefs, and desires to live life with a meaningful purpose. It captures the essence of who you are. A life mission statement is your personal "constitution." It expresses your unique personality, gifts, talents, abilities, dreams, and desires. Your life mission statement zeroes in on what makes you unique. It serves as a powerful catapult to launch you where you want to go (or don't want to go) in this tremendous life God has given you.

A life mission statement is an incredibly useful tool because it helps you make goals, plans, and decisions based on who you are and what's most important to you. It serves to help YOU live the life you want to live, not a life OTHERS think you should live.

Wow! A life mission statement . . . I know it sounds pretty intense, especially if you were just trying to decide whether to eat Top Ramen or Spaghetti-O's for dinner. But don't be intimidated by something so simple. A life mission statement is simply a series of statements about who you are and how you want to live your life.

My life mission statement reflects my highest values and desires for my life. What follows my life mission statement are my life goals, which will definitely take a lifetime to accomplish. My life goals reflect my most important priorities and relationships. It's where I want the majority of my time and energy to be spent. That includes such areas as my relationship with God, my wife, children, friends, career, and attitudes I choose to live by.

Do I always live up to my life mission statement? Not at all. At times, I fall shorter than a four-foot-five, three-hundred-pound Samoan high jumper trying to leap a six-foot bar, but that's where God's grace comes in. My life mission statement shows me, like God's Word, when I hit the marks I set for myself and when I miss them. I make an effort to read it every day. Think of your life mission statement as a sort of compass, a tool to guide you where you want to go. It's a powerful way to help you understand yourself and how to make the most of your life.

Your life mission statement will change over the course of your lifetime as *you* change, so don't think you've got to chisel this thing in stone. It will usually reflect the season of life you're in. When I read over Jeff's life mission statement, he focused on living a life of worship to the Lord. He included his desires to use his musical gifts for the Lord. Jeff listed his three to four personal strengths and weaknesses. He then wrote a number of personal goals that reflected his desire to serve in professional music ministry. Through writing his life mission statement, Jeff reflected who he is and who he wants to be.

From his life mission statement, Jeff has made specific decisions based on who God has made him to be and where he believes God is leading him. What's exciting about this process is that Jeff has turned down specific opportunities.

Why? Because they didn't match the values and priorities reflected in his life mission statement. That's a mark of maturity. When you can separate the bad decisions from the good decisions from the *best* decisions, then you put yourself in the strategic position of making the best decisions possible for your life. Don't just mosey through your life, make it a mission worth living.

The Step

Develop Your Life Mission Statement

Developing your life mission statement is an exciting process in becoming the person God has designed you to be. The key step to successful living is to integrate your relationship with God into all your gifts, talents, interests, activities, and relationships. *What you do flows out of who you are.* Your life mission statement reflects who you are and the person you want to grow to be. Answer the following set of questions to begin shaping your life mission statement and life goals. Don't feel pressured to finish this right away. It may take days, weeks, or even months to get your life mission statement down on paper, but the important thing is to start somewhere. Begin by praying to God for direction and insight. Ask him to reveal specific details to you about yourself. Ask him to show you how to develop dreams and lifelong goals that glorify him. Ask him to help you live your life on purpose, and for the grace to live according to his purposes.

1. Write down three to five of your greatest strengths.
2. Write down three to five of your greatest weaknesses.
3. What are your current activities and interests?

4. What are your current dislikes?
5. Describe five to eight characteristics of your personality.
6. What are your most important relationships?
7. What do you value most in life?
8. What are your most important priorities?
9. What are your spiritual gifts? (If you know what they are.)
10. What are you most passionate about?
11. What kind of lifelong goals would you like to set for yourself?
12. What dreams are worth your time and effort to pursue?
13. What are your most significant accomplishments?
14. What are the two or three areas of your life in which you want to excel?
15. How do you want to be remembered when you die?

What you've just done is develop a personal profile about yourself. Based on your responses, begin writing your life mission statement. Write short, clear sentences about your highest values and priorities. Don't worry if what you write doesn't seem profound. Identifying and clarifying your life mission is designed to be simple to read and simple to understand. You can begin by simply writing *My life mission is . . .*

If your passion is serving others, write down how you would like to live a life of service. If your relationships (God, friends, family) are most important to you, describe the qualities you want to live out in those relationships. Your life mission statement is what you make it, because it's a reflection of you. Your life mission statement will serve as a faithful guide to the important decisions you make in your life.

After writing your life mission statement, identify a number of lifelong goals you'd like to accomplish. Make them realistic, but be sure they're also a stretch. What are those things you want to spend the whole of your life pursuing? Again, write down statements that reflect the values and priorities most important to you. You could include a favorite verse of Scripture that describes your most important values. Write down attitudes, relationships, personal disciplines, and actions you are willing to commit to living. Your life mission statement is a tool designed to help you live successfully according to God's principles. Just like your life, your life mission statement is what you make it.

Discover Your Spiritual Gifts

The Story

Our tiny living room was packed with twelve hungry college students, surrounded by scrambled eggs, orange juice, blueberry muffins, and steaming cups of coffee. It was our weekly Friday morning Bible study and youth ministry staff meeting. Today was the day to go over the "Spiritual Gifts Assessments" everyone had filled out since our last meeting. We had a great team of college students who loved the Lord and were excited to serve high school students. I was eager to hear what each person had discovered.

After a short Bible study on spiritual gifts, each person began to share his or her discoveries. Peter had the gift of serving; he always enjoyed helping others. Like a pastor caring for his sheep, Gregg had the gift of shepherding and caring for others. Debbie was always saying positive, encouraging words to others; she had the gift of encouragement. Contagious with his faith, Ryan often shared the gospel with his friends and family; he had the gift of evangelism.

One after another, each student explained what they thought his or her spiritual gifts might be. Some were perplexed, others excited about their discoveries. As a ministry team, we encouraged and helped each other discover our spiritual gifts.

Serving. Helping. Encouraging. Teaching. Hospitality. Healing. Preaching. Pastoring. Wisdom. Knowledge. Faith. Leadership. Every Christian has been given spiritual gifts. Are you ready to discover how God wants to use you for his kingdom?

The Secret

> There are different kinds of gifts, but the same Spirit. There are different kinds of service, but the same Lord. There are different kinds of working, but the same God works all of them in all men.
>   Now to each one the manifestation of the Spirit is given for the common good.
>
> 1 Corinthians 12:4–7

God has designed you to be unique. You are an original. He has a special purpose for you—discover your uniqueness in Christ. He hasn't factory-made you to be a yakking cookie-cutter Christian who looks, talks, and acts like everyone else. You are not a clone . . . you are a gifted Christian.

God has given you spiritual gifts in order for you to make a unique contribution to the body of Christ. Spiritual gifts are not talents. They're not abilities or physical traits. Spiritual gifts are unique characteristics given to every believer for the purpose of building up the body of Christ. Just like their name, they are "gifts" and they are "spiritual" in nature.

Just as discovering your talent as an athlete, singer, or mechanic helps to shape your identity and view of yourself, discovering your spiritual gifts helps shape your identity in Christ. It can show you how you can contribute to God's work in other people's lives. It can show you how to make a major difference in the kingdom of God.

Just as the human body is created with hundreds of different parts and functions, God's church is made up of all sorts of unique parts. A spiritual gift assessment can help you figure out what part you are. More importantly, it can also help you understand what part you're not. A spiritual gift assessment is not a magical test to grade your level of spirituality or what a "neato" type person you are. It's just a tool. An instrument to inventory how God has wired you.

When you discover your spiritual gifts, you unlock a powerful way for the Holy Spirit to work in your life. You find out what you're equipped to do to serve others. You develop a stronger sense of identity in Christ and how he wants to use you in his kingdom. You discover your place in the body of Christ.

The Step

Get together with your youth pastor or college pastor and do a Bible study on spiritual gifts. Read Scripture passages on gifts (Rom. 12:4–8, 1 Cor. 12, Matt. 25:14–30) and discuss their implications. Then, go to a Christian bookstore and look for books on discovering your spiritual gifts. Find one with a spiritual gift inventory. Meet with a group of friends and make it a fun time for all to discover their spiritual gifts.

Direct Your Steps

The Story

With less than a half-mile to go in the 1994 twenty-fifth New York City Marathon, race leaders German Silva and Benjamin Paredes ran side by side toward the finish line. At Seventh Avenue and Fifty-ninth Street, Silva took a step, a turn that almost cost him the race. Instead of going straight like Paredes, Silva turned down Fifty-ninth Street, which was an escape route for media vehicles. Bad move. A very wrong turn.

Waving their arms and screaming at him, a number of bystanders yelled, "You're going the wrong way!"

His concentration broken, Silva looked up and realized his mistake. Making an abrupt about-face, he charged back up Fifty-ninth Street and reached the race route more than sixty yards behind Paredes. With less than four hundred meters to the finish line, Silva faced the longest (yet shortest) race of his life. He had a long way to go in an extremely short amount of time.

Breaking into a furious sprint, Silva charged toward Paredes in fierce determination to win. Fifty yards, forty yards, thirty yards . . . running uphill, Silva overtook Paredes less than three hundred yards from the finish and broke the finish line tape to victory. His wrong turn almost led to a second place finish. His right turn directed his steps to a hard-fought victory.

Even though Silva had been behind by sixty yards, his error in judgment didn't keep him from pushing on. After running twenty-six miles, he was determined not to let one mistake keep him from victory. Imagine the panic he felt when he realized his error; imagine the exhilaration he experienced when he broke the tape.

The Secret

> This is what the LORD says—your Redeemer, the Holy One of Israel: "I am the LORD your God, who teaches you what is best for you, who directs you in the way you should go.
>
> Isaiah 48:17

Wrong turns. Right turns. Developing a total life focus of following God begins with allowing the Lord to direct your steps. German Silva almost lost the New York City Marathon by taking a sudden wrong turn. Do you want your life to be filled with wrong turns and dead ends? Do you want to be a winner or loser in this life? Are you preparing for the victories God has planned for you? Or are you too busy to look where you're going?

Victory usually depends on the direction of your steps. Some students spend more time preparing for the prom than they do preparing for life. They don't know where they're going because they haven't planned on going anywhere. As you pray about the direction of your life, discovering your life purpose, and developing your life mission statement, you can count on God to lead you every step of the way. No matter what you choose to do in this life, what job you take, where you might live, whom you might marry, or what you will make of your life, God always promises to direct your steps.

Following Jesus is a lifelong process of learning God's best for you. What's best is found in his Word. He knows what you need in every step you take, every day of your life, so you can trust him with everything you have. At times, you'll pull a German Silva maneuver. You'll make plenty of wrong turns, but as you ask God for wisdom and direction you'll definitely make a whole bunch of right turns. Never be afraid to turn around when you discover you've made a wrong turn. God promises to point you in the right direction to the finish line where you'll find victory in Christ.

The Step

What direction would you like your life to be headed? Where would you like God to direct your steps? As you follow Christ, what are the greatest dreams and desires you'd like God to give you direction for? Go for a walk or a jog today and spend time praying about your life's direction. Ask God to direct every day of your life. Watch your step and believe that God knows what's best for you.

Partnering with Your Parents

The Story

You can save yourself a lot of hassle after you graduate from high school by beginning to partner with your parents in a few major life decisions. Though you may think your parents are clueless about a lot of things, there are many practical life skills you can learn from them—that is, if your parents are willing to partner with you. When I graduated from high school, even though I thought I was a stud for turning eighteen, I realize now that I was pretty stupid about how life worked.

I had never balanced a checkbook before. I didn't know anything about stocks, bonds, mutual funds, and investments. I didn't know a lick about how to get a car loan or how interest rates worked. I wasn't wary about the dangers of credit card debt and twenty-one-percent interest rollover rates. I had never applied for financial aid. I never had bought auto, medical, or dental insurance. No, my mother didn't dress me, but I wished I would have asked her and my dad a few more questions.

Fixing cars? I knew how to put air in the tires and where to add a can of oil. As an eighteen-year-old who thought he knew everything, I knew nothing. I could have learned a lot from my parents if I had been willing to ask and learn. My parents were encyclopedias of life experience from whom I could have gleaned all sorts of ideas, facts, wisdom, and knowledge.

What tasks and responsibilities in your immediate future are you facing that you have no clue about? How can you get the information you need to avoid making critical, careless mistakes? The first place to look is under your own roof. Your parents (even though you think they know less than the average Wheel of Fortune contestant) are a vital resource to your steps to success after high school.

The Secret

> My son, keep your father's commands and do not forsake your mother's teaching. Bind them upon your heart forever; fasten them around your neck. When you walk, they will guide you; when you sleep, they will watch over you; when you awake, they will speak to you.
>
> Proverbs 6:20–22

Before you find a partner for life, partner with your parents. Before you make a major career decision, partner with your parents. Before you find a business partner, partner with your parents. Abandoning your family in order to "find yourself" isn't all it's cracked up to be. Rather than pursuing the American myth of rugged individualism, I believe there's more wisdom in the saying, "There's strength in numbers." I've seen so many college-age people make unnecessary, careless, avoidable mistakes—all because they didn't know what they were getting themselves into. They could have easily said, "Hey, Dad, I've got a question." You have a lot to learn from your mom and dad.

If you have a poor relationship with your parents or if you come from an abusive family, then you're going to have to tweak what I say in this chapter by finding an older adult, an aunt, uncle, grandparents—someone you trust and respect—

to help you with your major life decisions. Whatever it takes, find a role model, a mentor, someone who will partner with you and help you through the stuff you've never done before.

The Book of Proverbs constantly speaks of the importance of learning from your parents and older, wiser people. I know it sounds extremely uncool and outright embarrassing, but you can save yourself a lot of headaches by asking your folks all the stuff I never asked mine. Learning from your folks makes you sharper, smarter, and savvy. It's what the Bible calls wisdom. God's plan for learning life lessons from your folks is designed to keep you from making foolish decisions. Ask questions. Talk with your parents. Be inquisitive. Take initiative. You'll be able to help all your friends who don't partner with their parents. Or, at least, those who wish they did.

The Step

Flip through the first ten chapters of Proverbs this week. Look for all the verses that talk about learning from your dad and mom. See what the Bible says about being wise and being foolish. Write down the characteristics you want to live by. Ask God to help you partner with your parents and lead a life of wisdom.

Partnering with Your Parents

Here's a checklist of ways you can partner with your parents after you graduate from high school. If your relationship with your parents isn't very good and you don't feel comfortable talking with them about these matters, be sure to find an older person you know and trust who can help you with these important areas of your life. Whatever you do, find someone who can be your partner as you strive for success after high school.

1. School/career development
2. Financial planning and cash control
3. Understanding insurance (auto, medical/dental, life)
4. Dating, relationships, and marriage
5. Goal-setting, priorities, time management
6. Starting your own business
7. Joining the military
8. Understanding rental and lease agreements
9. Choosing a roommate
10. How to communicate clearly to others
11. How to handle conflict
12. How to prepare a résumé and interview for a job
13. How to deal with a major life crisis
14. How to buy a car
15. Traveling Europe on a dollar a day (thirty days . . . that'd only cost your folks thirty bucks!)

Living under Your Parents' Roof without Going Insane

The Story

Throughout her high school years, Michelle had a fairly normal relationship with her mom and dad. She felt comfortable talking with them about almost any subject. Her parents always attended her athletic events and supported her younger siblings. Her brothers and sisters were usually tolerable, at least when they were asleep. Michelle's mom and dad were easygoing and relaxed. Until Michelle graduated from high school.

Once Michelle turned eighteen, it seemed that her parents became Dr. Jekyll and Mrs. Hyde. Michelle was a legal adult, and she didn't understand why her parents wanted to control her every move. *Have you thought about this . . . have you thought about that? What are you going to do with your life? Have you applied for the junior college yet? Where are you going tonight? What's his name? What time are you coming home?*

As a high school student, these were common questions Michelle was frequently asked, but she figured once she turned eighteen, her parents would back off. Not only did her parents not back off, they pressured her with constant demands, questions, and inquiries. Everything they said seemed to irritate her. Her little brothers and sisters were also driving her crazy. "I've got to get out of this house," Michelle told herself.

Michelle had no interest in attending the local junior college and, since she had no steady income, her only choice was to live at home. She had always wanted to be a hairstylist, so she enrolled in a beauty college downtown. "A hairstylist?" her parents gasped in surprise when she told them of her decision. "How can you make a living as a hairstylist?"

That was it. Michelle was sick of her parents policing her life, criticizing every decision she tried to make. If her parents couldn't accept her for who she was and let her pursue her own dreams, then she wanted out. She picked up the phone and called her best friend, who had an extra bedroom at her house. She asked if she could stay there until she could save enough money to move out on her own. Within an hour, Michelle was out the door. Uncharacteristically, she didn't even leave a note.

The Secret

> Live in harmony with one another. Do not be proud, but be willing to associate with people of low position. Do not be conceited. . . . If it is possible, as far as it depends on you, live at peace with everyone.
>
> Romans 12:16, 18

Michelle's story isn't unusual. Any young person who's tried to live at home after graduating from high school encounters problems to one degree or another. You will change. Your parents will change. What nobody really talks about, though, is how these changes will affect how you relate to one another. If you decide to live at home after high school, the challenge you face is how to live under your parents' roof without going insane.

Turning eighteen can change how you relate to your parents and how they relate to you in a number of ways. Your mom and dad have spent the past eighteen years raising, molding, guiding, shaping, and directing your life. The fact that you're now a legal adult doesn't always register in their minds. They're still used to telling you what to do and making sure you make the right decisions. *With you still around the house, they're not about to stop being the parents they've always been. They just can't turn their "parenting valve" off!*

Maybe your parents are divorced and you live with either your mom or dad, who've always been (despite the pressures of work and finances) as supportive as they could. Now that you're eighteen, they're ready for a break. They're ready for you to make your own decisions. Not only couldn't you wait until you turned eighteen, neither could they. You're on your own. Instead of acting like the parent your mom or dad has always been, he or she now just seems like a roommate. It makes you feel kinda weird.

Before you go insane and the men in white jackets come to take you to live in a padded room, applying God's Word to your life can be just what you need to live at peace with your parents. Living in harmony with your parents doesn't mean that there'll never be conflict. Being humble and willing to work with your parents will get you through the conflicts that are driving you crazy. Instead of living at home in a continual state of chaos, be willing to make adjustments in how you relate to your parents. Rather than claiming or demanding your rights as a legal adult, talk with your parents about their expectations and your own expectations. Work to set new ground rules for living together. As far as it depends on you, do what you can to live in peace with your parents. You can't change your parents, but you can change yourself. Making positive changes won't drive anyone insane, but it will promote peace in your home. That's a change worth going crazy for.

The Step

Hopefully you haven't stormed out of the house yet like Michelle did. If you're living at home with your parents, surprise them tonight by making a meal for them. Make a list of the things that bug you about living at home and talk to your folks about it. Work on setting mutual goals to keep peace in the house. Make the effort to pray with and for your parents. Pray for the peace with which God wants to fill your home. He promises to be with you even if you still feel like you're going insane.

Keeping in Touch

The Story

The next time you decide to go swimming off a sailboat, remember three things: (1) Take the sails down, (2) stay close to the boat, (3) don't go skinny-dipping.

Recently in my hometown of Dana Point, a sailor named Michael O'Connor (no relation to me . . . I think) rescued two swimmers he found stranded five miles out to sea. Earlier, O'Connor had sailed past an empty catamaran clipping along, heading to shore. Instead of trying to rescue the empty catamaran, he decided to take the opposite course in the hope of finding its former crew.

Immediately before calling the harbor patrol, O'Connor heard a faint cry for help. Two hundred yards away, he spotted two people frantically waving their arms and screaming. Keeping his eye on the two bobbing heads in the water, O'Connor sailed over to the two stranded swimmers. What he didn't know was that he was in for an interesting surprise.

When he pulled his boat alongside the two swimmers, he discovered that they both needed something more than a life preserver to wrap around themselves. The twenty-four-year-old man and his underage (seventeen years old) female companion were as naked as a merman and mermaid. Five miles out to sea . . . naked . . . with a twenty-four-year-old man . . . the catamaran heading to shore . . . how was the seventeen-year-old going to explain that one to her parents? No, I don't think the explanation about auditioning for a Disney sequel would have worked.

Lips blue with cold and shivering from hypothermia, the young couple struggled for forty-five minutes in the freezing water after forgetting to take down the catamaran's sails before their suitless swim—a very frigid faux pas.

The Secret

> The father of a righteous man has great joy; he who has a wise son delights in him. May your father and mother be glad; may she who gave you birth rejoice!
>
> Proverbs 23:24–25

Keeping in touch with your parents after high school doesn't have to be as difficult as swimming after a crewless catamaran. Keeping in touch is as simple as picking up a pen, the phone, typing a few keys on E-mail, or dropping by for a surprise visit when your parents least expect it. Seems simple, but making a consistent effort to keep in touch with your parents is harder than it sounds (calling home for money doesn't count).

You've probably spent the past eighteen years under your mom or dad's roof. Communication was usually possible (not that it always happened) by the mere fact of living in close proximity. Now that you're out of the house, your schedule is filled with classes, meetings, work schedules, road trips, and appointments to keep you and your folks out of touch. It's easy to let days turn into weeks and weeks into months. For the good of your relationship, both now and in the future, stay in touch. Call collect. Be novel and send *them* a care package (C.O.D., of course). Save some money and fly home on your mom's birthday. Be really adventurous and have one of them come and stay in your dorm room.

When you stay in touch with your parents, you give them the joy of knowing you're still interested in them. You give your folks a reason to rejoice in you. Even though there are a lot of messed up parents in this world, I believe many relationships could be healed by sons and daughters willing to take a risk to get involved with their parents' lives. You could be the one God wants to use to initiate healing in your relationship with your mom or dad. Give your parents a reason to have joy.

Wherever you go after high school, staying in touch with your parents is like staying close to the boat you've been sailing for the past eighteen years. It's easy to let important relationships get blown away by the gentle breezes of life.

When the storms of life rage, it's comforting to be close to the boat. Keeping your parents included in your life is one of the best ways to show how much you love them. It can also keep you from feeling naked, alone, and afraid. Parents are a wonderful covering. Stay close. Keep in touch.

The Step

You know what to do here with your parents . . . the ball is in your court!

Battling Your Family Baggage

The Story

Above my desk, next to my family photos of my wife and kids, is a grisly newspaper photograph I cut out from the sports page. It's a picture of two boxers, James Toney and Iran Barkley, battling it out in the ring. Though it's not a very good complement to the sweet and innocent pictures of my two smiling daughters, this tatter-edged boxing photo was too wild for me to pass up.

You can almost feel the photo reverberating. Firmly planted on Barkley's right jaw, Toney's fist jackhammers his opponent's face with deadly momentum. Crystal droplets of sweat are splashing all over the place. Barkley's bald head absorbs the blow like a Mack truck hitting a cement wall. Both bodies are glistening with a sweaty sheen. I'm surprised my desk is dry. There should be sweat all over it.

I'm not an avid boxing fan. Nor am I particularly fascinated with seeing people in pain. I keep this photo on my bulletin board as a reminder of the inner battles all Christians face with the "baggage" they carry in their lives. It's a reminder of the battles I know many college-age people go through with their families. Battling your family baggage is a fight you want to be prepared for after high school. It's no fun fighting against family members. It's also no fun battling what's going on inside of you. Maybe taking up boxing would be less painful. At least on the inside.

The Secret

> Therefore, there is now no condemnation for those who are in Christ Jesus, because through Christ Jesus the law of the Spirit of life set me free from the law of sin and death.
>
> Romans 8:1–2

Your family has a powerful impact on your relationship with God. Your relationship with your parents, brothers, and sisters can stimulate your growth in Christ. It can also sabotage it. Why? Because the baggage you carry with you from family problems can be a major distraction to your relationship with God.

If your mom or dad hasn't shown you unconditional love, you may at times feel like God doesn't love you. If you were constantly teased growing up, you may not believe that God seriously cares about you. Are your parents the silent type? Do you view God like a silent, aloof parent? Have your parents placed heavy, unrealistic expectations and constant performance measurements on your life? Do you live in fear of God giving you a spiritual report card as if you had to earn his approval? The hurt and pain you pick up from your family can load you down like a heavy, old beaten-up suitcase. Your inner struggles can become like a spiritual boxing ring where you fight your family baggage.

In Romans 7, Paul wrote about the inner battles he faced as a Christian. The good things he wanted to do, he didn't do. The bad things he didn't want to do, he did. Paul was locked in a boxing match between his old sinful nature and his new nature in Christ. He felt distracted. Frustrated. He knew his relationship with God was suffering because of this fight with all of his inner baggage.

God finally showed Paul, battle or not, family baggage or no family baggage, that there is no condemnation in Jesus Christ. He realized that he had been set free from the power of sin and death. In Christ Jesus, Paul was set free from his baggage.

If you're battling family baggage or just trying to survive your family problems one day at a time, realize that Jesus has set you free from your family baggage. You don't have to spend your life shadowboxing an unseen enemy. Sure, your family may still have problems; Jesus never promised to make your family perfect. He did, however, promise to give you peace. He did promise to give you strength to fight your battles. He did promise to set you free.

The Step

What kind of family baggage do you carry? Instead of dealing with family problems in a positive, healthy way, some people choose to blame their family members. Instead of blaming, why don't you hand over any family baggage to God? Ask God to set you free from the baggage you battle. Ask him to give you wisdom to know how to live in peace with your family (if that's possible!). You can trust God to walk with you in your family problems. Your battles are his battles. His peace is your peace.

Making a Crux Move

The Story

"Falling! Take!" I frantically screamed to Todd, my climbing partner, as I began to tumble down the steep granite slope. The first word explained my obvious relationship between the rope, the three-hundred-foot route we were climbing, and gravity; the second meant to take in as much slack in the rope as possible, thus minimizing my plummet from twenty feet to fifteen.

This was my fourth winger (fall). Todd and I were climbing "Gold Nugget," a classic five-star route on Suicide Rock in Idylwild, California. The difficulty rating was only a 5.10 (moderately difficult), one of many that we had previously climbed. However, the route was first rated in 1974, and we were climbing it twenty years later. Worn smooth over the past twenty years, it had to at least be rated over 5.11. I had never fallen so much in my life. I already had one twenty-five-foot fall, two twenty-footers, and my latest fifteen-foot body slammer. Even though I knew that falling was one of the primary dangers to avoid in rock climbing, this route was testing me like no other climb I'd experienced. Sick of being a human bowling ball, I was determined to not let this route keep beating me up.

Climbing back to the bolt and carabiner, my last protection placement, I caught my breath and looked for any dime-size holds I could dig my fingernails into. As I looked up the massive grey slope above me, I could hear the quiet mountain wind whispering through the pine trees. Shifting my heavy rack of gear around my back, I felt like an exhausted cat attempting to climb a pane of smooth glass. Looking down at Todd seventy feet below me, I yelled, "climbing," edged my left foot on a slight depression in the rock, dug my fingers onto the slope, and pressed on toward the crux. The hardest part of the climb was yet to come.

The Secret

> Listen, my son, accept what I say, and the years of your life will be many. I guide you in the way of wisdom and lead you along straight paths. When you walk, your steps will not be hampered; when you run, you will not stumble. Hold on to instruction, do not let it go; guard it well, for it is your life.
>
> Proverbs 4:10–13

The most difficult move on any climbing route is the crux move. Whether a route is filled with cracks, large or small handholds, difficult traverses, or intimidating overhangs, the whole route is rated according to the most difficult move. If your ability, skill, and stamina can't get you past the crux move, you shouldn't climb the route. Unless, of course, you want to put yourself and others in serious danger.

When you graduate from high school, at one point or another, you are going to face a serious crux move—moving away from your parents. Depending on your parents, family history, or future plans, a crux move is a big change you might eagerly await or secretly dread.

"I can't wait to get out of this house," has been the marching cry of millions of teenagers. Getting out is easy; staying out is the hard part. Before you make the crux move of living on your own or with friends, make sure you have all the necessary climbing protection you need: adequate financial support (either your folks or yourself), a job to pay the onslaught of new expenses you'll have, someone to live with that you know and trust (I know young people who've gotten slammed for ex-roommates' rent, utility bills, etc.), and a game plan to fall back on in case things don't work out. A crux move can bring you the freedom and independence you've always wanted, but beware, moving out of your parents' home can bring headaches and financial hardships you never imagined. Take *moi* for example. I once arrived home after a week's vacation to find the locks on my apartment changed, three roommates gone, and a note on the door from the landlord. Before I knew what had happened, I was back on my parents' doorstep paying rent to them!

One thing I love about God's Word is its constant plea to get wisdom, understanding, counsel, and knowledge. It directs you and me to be smart, not stupid, in every move we make with our lives. Before you make a crux move, examine all the pros and cons, talk to your parents, find out about the laws regarding rent on an apartment or condo, make a sample budget to see if you can cover all your expenses, and, above all, don't move in with just anyone. Convenience can create chaos quicker than a speedy slide down a steep rock. Walk in the direction of God's Word. Hold on to his instructions for your life. If you're thinking about making a crux move, he'll give you the wisdom to decide where your next step should be.

The Step

If you're planning to move out of your parents' home in the near future, what are your reasons for doing so? Knowing your reasons for making a crux move can keep you from making a move you might later regret. It can also help you benefit from the confidence that comes from making a good decision. Whether you're joining the military, moving out on your own, or going to college, take the important step of knowing why you're moving out. Amazingly enough, it's a step some people never consider.

Backward Living
in a Fast-Forward
World

Living with the Author of Change

The Story

Chances are that by the time you read this book, you've already been cured of your senioritis . . . you've already graduated (oh yeah, I haven't even said "Congratulations" yet, and this book is almost over! How rude of me!). Do you remember your senioritis symptoms? Senioritis plagues millions of high school students all over America each year. A number of high school seniors were recently asked what their definition of senioritis is.

"Total lack of willingness to do much of anything important" (Dan, eighteen).

"Relaxing in class and having fun, but also having a fear that I may never see my high school friends again" (Mark, eighteen).

"A lack of willingness to think intellectually" (Andy, eighteen).

"A state of confusion and not wanting to deal with school because you're worrying about college" (Alevya, eighteen).

"Senioritis makes you fall asleep first period, second period, third period . . ." (Alan, eighteen).

"The ability to do good work, but also being too lazy to do it" (Greg, eighteen).

"Finding every reason not to come to school" (Stephanie, seventeen).

"Being all-consumed by that one single glorious day when one graduates . . . Vegetating until that moment" (Arthur, eighteen).

The Secret

I am making everything new!

Revelation 21:5

Senioritis is a symptom that means you're dying for change and the only real cure is getting out of high school. The only problem with some people is that they live with senioritis the rest of their lives. They're always waiting for change. Waiting for life to get better. Hoping that somehow, somewhere, sometime, something in their life will soon change. They live in a sort of perpetual laziness, expecting God to drop a big bundle of contentment in their laps while they channel surf for five hours, ignoring what needs changing in their lives. If there's one thing you want to get over as soon as possible when you leave high school, it's senioritis.

People who live with sustained senioritis are never content. Their attitudes go something like this, "When I graduate from college, then I'll arrive." "When I land the perfect job, then I'll be really happy." "When I find the ultimate mate for life, then I'll be fulfilled." The next car, the next house, the vacations, the kids. Happiness, contentment, and peace are always "out there." They never "arrive."

Change in this life is inevitable. Living with God, the author of change, is your most important relationship to help you through the changes you'll face. Instead of expecting your world, your circumstances, your outer life after graduation to change, let God make the real changes that count—changes in your heart.

When I find myself struggling with decisions about my life, my attitudes, my relationships, my circumstances, or my future, I soon discover that what's outside of me doesn't need to change. What's inside me needs to change. I need to change. *I need God to change me.* It usually takes me a while to discover that God doesn't necessarily want to change my outer world. He wants me to receive his grace and allow him to change my inner world. That's where I discover the peace and contentment of Christ. While I'm waiting around, tapping my fingers, wondering why God hasn't changed my circumstances, Jesus seems to be standing next to me waiting for me to yield control to him. "Are you ready?" he asks; "Are you ready to give up control? Are you ready to start looking at life from my perspective instead of your perspective?" Am I ready? Are you? Living with the author of change is a change worth making every day.

The Step

Are you willing to give up control of your life? Are you ready to totally place all of your plans, dreams, and circumstances in God's hands? What kinds of inner changes do you think God would like to make in your life? Take a bold, giant step in your life today by giving God control of your life. He promises to make the necessary changes to bring you closer to him.

You Are a Masterpiece in the Making

The Story

At the Accademia Museum in Florence, Italy, the world famous statue of Michelangelo's eighteen-foot-tall David is an artistic wonder. *Grolier's New Word Encyclopedia* explains the magnetic mystery behind this sculptured stud. "Depicted just before his historic battle with Goliath, David reveals a psychologically charged state of mind that is reflected in the contrapposto of his pose." I couldn't have said it better myself, but I think the real reason why Michelangelo's *David* is so popular is because Michelangelo dared to carve an eighteen-foot-tall naked man. No wonder Goliath lost . . . would you want to go into battle against a naked man?

I'm no art buff, but David isn't the most amazing sculpture I've ever seen. My favorite sculptures are Michelangelo's uncompleted masterpieces—the four, unfinished works called the "Slaves," which I passed by on my way to gawk at the completed, perfect David. Each a separate block of white marble, Michelangelo's slaves are twisted, contorted, half-finished men, frozen in their uncompleted states.

As I stood admiring these eternal prisoners, their bent, turning bodies seemed to be locked in an eternal struggle to wrestle out of the stone. The straining, desperate looks on their faces revealed torturous centuries of hopelessness. Hunchbacked, pockmarked, and rough with a coarse, gritty texture, the slaves are the artistic opposite of the soft, white, stately, smooth texture of David. The slaves are ugly. David is a handsome, beautiful work of art. As I walked around each of the massive slaves, I was tempted to grab a chisel and hammer. I wanted to set them free.

The Secret

> In all my prayers for all of you, I always pray with joy because of your partnership in the gospel from the first day until now, being confident of this, that he who began a good work in you will carry it on to completion until the day of Christ Jesus.
>
> Philippians 1:4–6

I can't relate to David very well. He's perfect. Taller than me. A giant killer. Works a mean sling. He struts around, uh, well, um, you know . . . naked. The slaves? Now there's a group of guys that don't have it all together. I've got a lot in common with them. Do you?

As a Christian you are an unfinished work of art. You're a masterpiece in the making. As you probably realize more than anyone else, God has a lot more work to do in your life. That's the kind of healthy spiritual attitude to accept when you're tempted to think you should be finished by now. You and I are just like those unfinished slaves with one big, hunking exception—Michelangelo didn't get around to finishing these four marble masterpieces, *God promises to never stop working on you.* The master sculptor is in the continual, daily process of carving you into the image of his son, Jesus Christ. If you feel like you're supposed to have it all together now that you're out of high school, lighten up the chisel blows on yourself.

As a young Christian, Philippians 1:4–6 was one of my favorite Bible passages. It still is and here's why: in order to keep walking with Christ, every Christian needs to be continually reminded of God's continued work in his or her life. Living in an "insta-everything" society, we tend to expect change to come quickly. We forget that real, lasting inner changes take a long time. They're the type of character-building changes only God can carve. We expect a masterpiece to be whipped out in a few quick minutes rather than accept the slow, gentle, deliberate work of the Master.

What do you wish you could change quicker about yourself? Is it patience you struggle with? You feel like peeling your new roommate's eyelids over his face every time he complains how rotten life is? How about your friends who go away to school while you have to stay at the local junior college? Do you wrestle with envy and jealousy over how easy life seems to go for them? How do you keep your heart from becoming a heart of stone?

If you feel you "should" be a spiritually perfect David, but really feel like an imprisoned slave, then step back and look at what David was really like. Though he was the only person in the Bible that was called "a man after God's own heart," David had his share of spiritual disasters. Adultery. Murder. Deception. Poor parenting skills. Though David had many victories, he was hardly a finished piece of art. I don't care what art critics say about his antipasto contrapposto, David had a long way to go. David was an unfinished follower of God. Just like you. Just like me.

Reminding yourself that you are a masterpiece in the making will help you put things into perspective when the devil whispers one of his deceptive lies about you standing on some pedestal in a world famous museum. Your friends and family will not be impressed if you try to come off perfect. Your walk with God will be much more authentic if you simply allow yourself to be a work in progress. Get out of the way. Let God do his work in your life. Allow yourself to be a masterpiece in the making. Don't be enslaved to sin or to the person you think you should be. You're the one God wants to set free.

The Step

Visit a museum this week. Find out how long it took for some of the masterpieces to be completed. What were some of the techniques used by the master artists? How are these techniques similar to what God wants to do in your life? Write down two or three areas in your life on which you'd like God to put his hands to work. What kind of progress in your life do you see so far?

23

Waiting on God Even When It Hurts

The Story

As a high school volleyball player at Laguna Beach High School, Kit was an outstanding athlete. After playing volleyball at Orange Coast Junior College, she transferred to the University of Oregon to play volleyball for the Ducks. Kit was looking forward to a successful season and the excitement of playing Division I volleyball. Until she woke up one morning and couldn't get out of bed.

What began as a nagging pain in her ring finger on her left hand a year earlier soon became a debilitating, painful disease. Kit went to a doctor and discovered that she had rheumatoid arthritis. The pain in her left hand had spread to her arms, legs, hips, and eventually to her whole body. Because of her intense pain, Kit returned home from the University of Oregon in disappointment.

Only a year earlier, Kit was jumping, blocking, digging, and spiking volleyballs all across the court. Now she could barely get out of bed in the morning. For the first year of her disease, her body ached constantly. At times, her arthritis became so painful that it was impossible for her to walk. To ease the throbbing pain, her father picked her up and carried her into a Jacuzzi where she could soak her inflamed joints. As she explained her condition, Kit said, "My whole body feels like a sprained ankle."

Through this discouraging, painful disease, Kit has had to learn how to wait on God. She's visited numerous doctors and tried various sorts of healing remedies. She recently had to have surgery on one of her wrists because of the arthritis. Her family, friends, and elders at her church have constantly prayed for healing, asking God to perform a miracle. So far, no miracle has come. Kit is still waiting on God. She's still having to endure her pain every day. She is waiting to be healed. She is waiting on God even when it hurts.

The Secret

> I waited patiently for the LORD; he turned to me and heard my cry. He lifted me out of the slimy pit, out of the mud and mire; he set my feet on a rock and gave me a firm place to stand. He put a new song in my mouth, a hymn of praise to our God. Many will see and fear and put their trust in the LORD.
>
> Psalm 40:1–3

People like Kit amaze me. Facing intense, crippling pain almost every day of her life, she refuses to get bitter and blame God for her physical condition. On some days, she limps along as if she got hit by a truck, but she always seems to have a smile on her face. That doesn't mean she never struggles in her faith. She's often tempted to doubt if God knows what's best for her. Kit has spent hours in prayer without answers, days in bed without comfort, and years of wondering if she will have to live like this for the rest of her life. And yet, through all her pain, she has chosen to faithfully wait on God.

What is your response when you are forced to wait on God? Does your relationship with God change when he doesn't get back to you right away? What have you prayed about lately for which you haven't received any answer from God? Waiting on God, even when it hurts, tests your faith, your character, your very relationship with him. Waiting on God is a true test of your love and commitment to Christ. It's God's way of strengthening your trust in him. It's his way of carving your character into the character of Jesus Christ.

Just like a little kid running up and down the aisles of Toys R Us begging his or her parents for the latest what-chamacallit gizmo toy, it's hard to wait on God when your requests seem perfectly legitimate. *Lord, I need money to pay for my school tuition. Lord, please help me to find a job so I can pay rent. God, help my sister to get off drugs. Jesus, please heal this disease in my body.* Waiting on God can seem like torture, but is God like a medieval torturer? If God always met your every need when you requested his immediate response, would you ever have a real need for him? Or would God just be your personal valet? Waiting on God, though it's a difficult lesson, is a reminder of who is in ultimate control. It's God's way of saying, "Don't just wait on me; rest in me. I hear your cries. I see your pain. I will be your strength in weakness. My grace is sufficient for you."

God promises to pull you out of the slimy pit you're waiting in. From the tests and trials he brings you through, he will give you a new place to stand. From where you will stand, you will have a new perspective. You will see your circumstances differently than the way you saw them when you were in the pit. From cries of desperation, he'll give you songs of praise to him. You will discover God's purposes for making you wait so long. Those are lessons only you can learn. No one can teach them to you. No one can do your waiting on God for you. He is in the process of shaping your life into the life of his son. Even Jesus had to wait on his Father. In the Garden of Gethsemane, Jesus had to live with unanswered prayers. On the cross, Jesus had to die with unanswered prayers. Jesus had to wait on God even when it hurt.

The Step

In what areas of your life are you waiting on God right now? Do you know someone who is living with unanswered prayer like Kit? What do you think are God's purposes for making you wait on him? Write what you think those reasons are and ask God to give you the patience and strength to keep waiting on him. He has your best interests in mind. His purposes for your life are best discovered by waiting on him.

24

How Will You Be Remembered?

The Story

Bill Murray is one of my favorite comedians. I loved him in *Ghost Busters, Caddyshack, Scrooged, Groundhog Day,* and *What About Bob?* Bill Murray isn't only funny in the movies, he's also a scream on the golf course.

Last week I watched Bill Murray on television playing golf at the Pebble Beach Pro Am. He's an absolute clown on the course. He's probably broken every rule ever written on golf etiquette. With all other golfers wearing nice, expensive clothes in this prestigious tournament, Bill Murray wore thrift clothes with a dorky golf hat. Every year, he has the largest gallery following him. At Pebble Beach, one of the most beautiful golf courses in the world, Bill Murray drags into sandpits old ladies who trip and fall while he pulls them down the sandy slopes. He cracks jokes while others are concentrating and trying to tee off.

His professional partner, Scott Simpson, has seen score-cards full of Bill Murray's course antics. Interviewed by a reporter, Simpson was asked to remember his favorite Bill Murray golf antic. "It might be a round at Kapalua (Hawaii). Bill is teeing it up, about to hit, and three ladies yell, 'Bill, give us something to remember you by.'

"They yell again, 'Bill, give us something to remember you by.' Bill drops his clubs, goes over to one of the ladies, takes a wad of gum out of his mouth, and sticks it on one of the ladies' foreheads." *A great shot, a truly great shot.*

I'm sure Bill will be remembered for making millions of people laugh. How will you be remembered?

The Secret

In the night I remember your name, O LORD, and I will keep your law.

Psalm 119:55

I was sixteen years old when I dedicated my life to Jesus Christ. When I went to my high school five-year reunion, it was basically like any other college party. There were four options. You either: (1) Worked and chose not to go to college; (2) Had just graduated from college; (3) Were still in college; (4) Were married (with or without kids). I remember talking with a girl I vaguely remembered from high school. I was twenty-three at the time and nearly choked on an ice cube when she told me she was married with two kids. I didn't even have a girlfriend!

Five years later, my wife and I didn't bother going to my ten-year reunion because it was too expensive. But even though my twenty-year reunion is a long way away, I'm planning to go to it. By God's grace, I'm planning on being remembered as the same as I was in high school. Of course, my life has changed and my friendship with God has changed over the years, but I'm grateful for God's faithfulness to keep me walking with him. At my twenty-year reunion, I don't want people to see *me* as much as I want them to see God's faithfulness in my life.

How do you want to be remembered? That is a critical question for you to wrestle with. I believe how we pray and plan for the future has a radical impact on who we are today. It affects our priorities, relationships, our decisions, our thoughts, habits, strengths and weaknesses.

Do you want to be remembered for remembering God? Do you want your former classmates at your twenty-year reunion to discover that you're still a Christian? Do you want them to be amazed at God's faithfulness in your life? Granted, a lot of people won't be amazed or give a rip about your relationship with God, but God can use your life for a very special purpose twenty years from now if you're willing to remain faithful to him. In between all those years, you'll continue to experience his unconditional love, peace, forgiveness, grace, and strength. Those are qualities worth remembering. Your friendship with God will flourish if you don't forget him. God's promises are something you never, ever want to forget. Forget your locker combo. Forget your teachers' names. Forget all those dates and places you memorized in History class, but don't forget God. Stick that thought on your forehead.

The Step

Write down ten things you want to be remembered for. List your commitments, personal qualities, and whatever is most important to you today. Now, what steps can you take today to live these things out in your life? Ask God for his strength to always remember your commitment to him.

Living Life Backwards

The Story

At my desk, where I spend the majority of my time writing books and articles, I have a quote on a small piece of paper that sits at the bottom of my computer screen. If you've ever spent time on one of these stupid machines typing reports, projects, term papers, books, articles, poetry, or personal journals, you'll appreciate the appropriateness of this quote:

> IT'S GONE.
> AND YOU DIDN'T BACK IT UP.

That little piece of paper is just the reminder I need. Backing up my writing work on a small, fifty-cent floppy disk takes only seconds to do, but the mental tenacity it takes me to remind myself to do it is tremendous. A simple task, but a monumental effort. My computer is my best friend and worst enemy. I have lost whole chapters of books, manuscript proposals, pages of writing ideas, and research projects for school by failing to do what every computer manual says to do: *Back it up.* You want to see a grown man cry? Pull the plug on my computer while I'm tappin' away. I have broken into tears more than once at the loss of weeks' worth of work. It's one of the sickest, stomach-churning feelings I know.

Small children. Power surges. Electrical storms. Even cats can create computer chaos. I never thought I could kill a cat, but one day while I was working on a writing project, my daughter's kitty, Whoops-A-Daisy, started playing with the electrical cord to my computer and yanked it out of the socket. *Zap!* My computer screen went blank. My darkest thoughts considered a million cat execution scenarios for at least half a second. Okay, maybe more like ten seconds. Cats and computers just don't mix. They can both drive you to do crazy things. That cat was graciously spared one of its nine lives.

The Secret

> Brothers, I do not consider myself yet to have taken hold of it. But one thing I do: Forgetting what is behind and straining toward what is ahead, I press on toward the goal to win the prize for which God has called me heavenward in Christ Jesus. . . . Only let us live up to what we have already attained.
>
> Philippians 3:13–14, 16

If you've just lost your research paper on medieval pheasant hunting and you didn't back it up, kiss it good-bye. There's nothing you can do to retrieve it. It's in computer heaven and you're stuck staring at a blank screen. The same is true with your life. Once your life is over, it's gone, and there's nothing you can do to get it back. Your life is a gift from God and you are given one shot at life here on terra firma. Uno. No matter what good intentions you have about making something of your life, about somehow making a difference in this world, if you don't do it now, there's nothing you can do to back it up. Once your life is over, you can't back it up.

Living life backwards is my weird way of thinking how I want to live forwards. Since I know I can't back up my life, I often think about how I want to live my life today and in the future. I picture myself as an old man looking back on my life, reflecting how I spent my days here on earth. I look at my relationship with God to see if it's still growing and alive. I look at the quality of my relationships with my wife, my kids, my extended family, and my closest friends. I ask myself if I've been faithful to God and the people most important to me. I look to see if my life is filled with regret, broken promises, and secrets. Or have I experienced peace, satisfaction, and God's abundant grace in knowing he has used me in small ways to make a meaningful difference for his kingdom? Living life backwards is my way of backing up my life. It causes me to consider who I want to be in Christ in spite of who I am today. Living life backwards gives me a big picture perspective of what matters most.

Backing up your life begins with forgetting about the sins and struggles of your past, setting your eyes on the future and pressing on to the life in Christ God has called you to. If you can do that every day of your life, you'll be a true success. No matter what it costs, straining ahead to win the prize of heaven will be worth far more than any achievement, status, or material possession you accumulate here on earth. You'll be able to look back on your life someday and have no regrets. You'll look back and thank God for making something beautiful out of your life. You'll be amazed, truly amazed, at the grace and faithfulness he showered on you every step of the way.

Graduating with God is living up to what you've already attained in Christ Jesus. It's saving, backing up, what you already have experienced with Jesus and pressing on to the next phase of your life. It means going forward with God even though your friends may be going backward. It's running ahead to God instead of away from God. If you want to have a truly successful life, a wonderful life experiencing all of God's best for you, begin living backwards today. Live today how you want to look back on your life in the future. If you do, you'll have no regrets. Only rejoicing.

The Step

Living life backwards is a giant step to success after high school. Take the next few minutes to pretend you're eighty years old. Look back over your life. What do you want your relationship with God to look like? What do you want your relationships with your family, your spouse, and your kids to be like? What would you like to have accomplished in life? What will your single greatest contribution be? How will you know you've made a difference? Now write down the qualities, characteristics, goals, and dreams you have for living your life backwards today. How will you live today to be the person you want to look back on and see?